NatuRe CRafts

Joy Williams

NORTH LIGHT BOOKS

cincinnati, ohio
artistsnetwork.com

ABOUT THE AUTHOR

Joy Williams resides on the near North side of Chicago with her husband Joel and their newest addition, Pearl. Joy's unique creations reflect many years of teaching arts and crafts to urban children at summer camps along with directing art classes at an inner-city private school.

Joy finds her **inspiration** in the faces of her students.

The author at age 10!

Nature Crafts. © 2002 by Joy Williams. Manufactured in China. All rights reserved. No part of this book may be reproduced in any form or by any electronic or mechanical means including information storage and retrieval systems without permission in writing from the publisher, except by a reviewer, who may quote brief passages in a review. Published by North Light Books, an imprint of F&W Publications, Inc., 4700 East Galbraith Road, Cincinnati, Ohio 45236. (800) 289-0963. First edition.

Other fine North Light Books are available from your local bookstore or art supply store or direct from the publisher.

06 05 04 03 02   5 4 3 2 1

Library of Congress Cataloging-in-Publication Data
Williams, Joy
    Nature Crafts / by Joy Williams.
        p. cm.
    ISBN 1-58180-292-7 (alk. paper)
        1. Nature Craft—Juvenile Literature. 2. Nature Craft. 3. Handicraft. I. Title
    TT157 .W572 2002
    745.5 21

2001058701

Editors: Maggie Moschell and Kathi Howard
Designer: Andrea Short
Layout Artist: Kathy Gardner
Production Coordinator: Mark Griffin
Photographer: Christine Polomsky

THANK YOU...

first of all, I want to thank God for allowing me to do what I enjoy most, sharing my art with children. Much, much thanks to my editor Maggie Moschell, who has been such an encouragement and source of talent. Thanks to Debbie Baumgartner for her ideas and computer skills. Andrea Spicer—where do I begin? Jannelle Schoonover, my most wonderful sister, thanks for another belly full of laughs. Also thanks to my super parents, Royce and Carol Schoonover; the best in-laws, Vic and Katherine Williams; and Bethie Wagler, Tammy Perlmutter, Tiana Clark, Deb Strahan, Corey Escue, Karen Warne, Marsha Spaniel, Eric Bixler, Kat Seiler, Georgia Coleman, all of the students at U.C.S. and my family and friends at J.P.U.S.A. for their support.

dedication

This book is dedicated to my husband Joel

and our Pearl of great price.

I love you both!

A NOTE TO GROWN-UPS

As an art teacher, one of my favorite times to teach children is at outdoor summer camp. Children love to collect things that they find as they walk in the woods, and they think it's fun to use these "treasures" to create one-of-a-kind craft projects. Best of all, sticks, rocks, shells, pinecones, and seeds are free and fun to find.

Encouraging Budding Artists

A kitchen counter or table is a good location for making arts and crafts because it's near a sink and spills can easily be cleaned up. Paper, paint, glue, scissors, paintbrushes, crayons, an art shirt and other odds and ends can be stored in boxes under a cabinet or other accessible place so that your child can easily take things out and put them away any time the creative urge strikes.

Each project is both fun to do and educational. Clear step-by-step photos with instructions and materials lists are provided so that your child can do the projects with little adult help. There are many creative ways to complete each project.

Collecting Supplies

Before sending your small scavenger outdoors to hunt for materials, you will want to discuss safety and ecology regarding your particular neighborhood. You may want to explain why it's not a good idea to collect large rocks from someone's landscaped yard, why a bird's nest with eggs should remain undisturbed or how to identify poison ivy or other nasty plants.

An outing to a park is an enjoyable way to look for materials together. Be sure that you are acquainted with the rules regarding removal of natural materials. Most nature preserves, state parks and national parks do not allow people to take anything home with them.

The good news is that nature is truly all around us, not only in the woods or at the beach. The perfect leaf for a print may be found in a parking lot, a gorgeous rock might be lying in the gutter. I hope that this book will inspire you and your child to take an extra trip into the forest, a walk on the beach or even a closer look into your own backyard to discover all of the unique and beautiful creations that nature sets out for us.

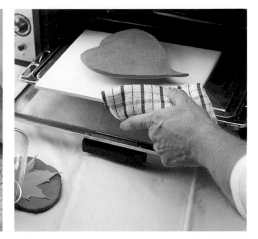

rt and craft projects can be messy. over your workspace with paper or vinyl tablecloth.

Wipe up any spills right away and always clean up when you are finished.

Follow the directions carefully for each project. Ask an adult for help when you need it or when the directions say that an adult must help.

eck with an adult to be sure that u are allowed to gather materials y place that's not your own yard. ther sticks from the ground instead breaking off live tree branches.

Take only what you think you'll use. Your leftover natural materials can go right back where you found them.

NATURAL MATERIALS

If you can't find the things you need in your own yard, look in these places:

THE WOODS

- Leaves from trees and bushes
- Twigs and sticks
- Acorns and seed pods
- Pinecones and pine needles
- Pebbles and rocks
- Flowers

THE BEACH

- Empty shells
- Sea horses
- Starfish
- Beach glass
- Driftwood
- Sand

CREEKS AND RIVERS

- Pebbles and rocks
- Twigs and sticks
- Flowers

GARDEN STORES

- Birdseed
- Bags of rocks and gravel
- Ferns and flowers
- Potting soil
- Grass seeds

CRAFT STORES

- Raffia
- Dried plants
- Feathers
- Dried and pressed flowers
- Shells and beach glass

OTHER SUPPLIES

Here are some of the supplies you will use most often:

PAPERS

Some projects look better with paper that you can see through. Other papers you can use in your projects include:

- **Tagboard** is smooth, stiff paper that is good for making cards and bookmarks.

- **White writing paper (copier paper)** is good for making leaf rubbings because it's thin.

- **Construction paper** can be used for most of the projects.

GLUES

Choose the type of glue best for each project:

- **White glue** can be used for most projects.

- **Tacky glue** is a thicker white glue best used for gluing bumpy objects such as rocks.

- **Decoupage medium** coats and protects fresh leaves and other objects used in your projects. White glue mixed with a little water can be used in place of decoupage medium.

CLAYS

Some clays need to be baked in a conventional oven or a toaster oven. Ask an adult to bake projects for you and follow the directions on the package.

- **Polymer clay** must be baked and can be used to make a mold for beads.

- **Oven-bake clay** must be completely dry before an adult bakes it.

- **Air-dry clay** comes in white or black and doesn't need to be baked.

PAINTS

These are the paints you will need for your nature projects:

- **Watercolor paints** can be used to put color on a shell, stain a stick or paint on paper.

- **Tempera or acrylic paint** mixed with water can be used in place of watercolors.

- **Fabric paint** is used for making prints on fabric because it doesn't wash out. You can also use acrylic paint for painting on fabric.

Leaving Your Mark

LOOKING FOR A QUICK AND EASY GIFT for your friends, parents or teacher? Start by collecting and pressing your favorite kinds of flowers and leaves. Then use colored paper and contact paper to make bookmarks.

IMPATIENS

OCRE GRANDE

● **PUNCH A HOLE** in the top and tie on a piece of raffia or yarn to finish your bookmark.

SUPPLIES

pressed flowers and leaves

clear contact paper

tagboard or construction paper

scissors

HOW TO PRESS FLOWERS AND LEAVES

Collect different ferns, flowers and leaves and place them *between* the pages of a thick *book*, such as a phone *book*. Let it sit for two to three weeks. Handle the pressed plants carefully or they will break.

Cut the tagboard or other paper to the size and shape want for your bookmark. For ety, choose paper with different rns and colors. Arrange your sed plants on the paper.

2. Cut enough clear contact paper to cover both sides of the bookmark, plus a little extra. Peel the paper from the back of the contact paper and place it sticky side down on top of the bookmark.

3. Turn the bookmark over and fold the rest of the contact paper onto the back. Press out all the air bubbles with your fingers then trim the edges with scissors.

Seashell Garden

THIS PROJECT USES A LARGE SHELL TO GROW A SMALL GARDEN in about a week! If your shell is large enough, you can try growing small flowers, too. Add a face on your shell for even more fun.

KIDS! Try this too!

● **GREAT REFRIGERATOR MAGNETS** are easy to make by gluing a small magnet on the back of a shell.

SUPPLIES

grass seeds

potting soil

large shell

Plus you need:

• spray bottle with water

tip

When the grass needs to be cut, use scissors to "mow" it.

1. Fill a shell three-fourths of the way full of soil.

2. Spread a lot of grass seed on top of the soil.

3. Cover the seeds with a thin layer of soil and place the shell near a sunny window. Keep the soil moist until the grass spouts. Then water it daily.

Leaf Paintings

Y OU CAN CREATE BEAUTIFUL LEAF PICTURES two different ways in

this project using crayons or watercolor paint. With an assortment of leaves and

different kinds of paper you can make greeting cards, gift tags, wrapping or just

hang up your painting on the wall to enjo

SUPPLIES

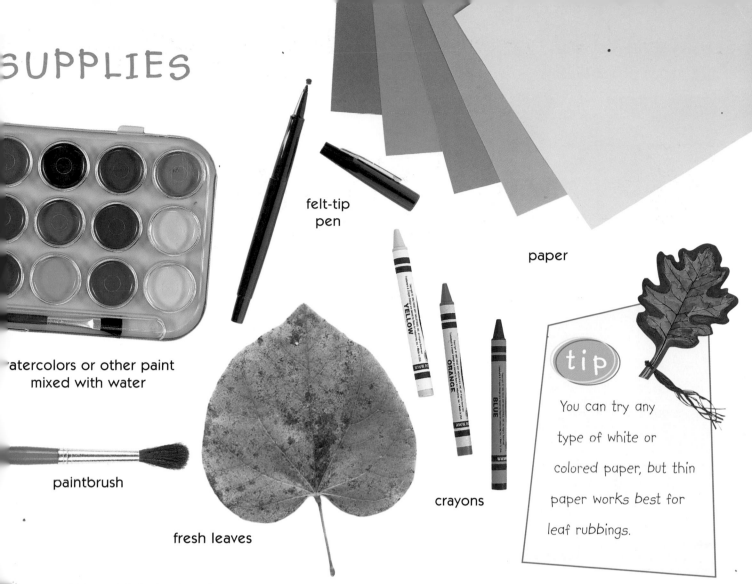

felt-tip pen

paper

watercolors or other paint mixed with water

paintbrush

fresh leaves

crayons

tip

You can try any type of white or colored paper, but thin paper works best for leaf rubbings.

CRAYON RUBBING LEAVES

Put a leaf under a piece of paper with the veins up.

2. Hold the paper down with one hand and use the side of a crayon to rub over the leaf with your other hand. Make sure the paper and leaf stay put.

3. Paint over the entire paper with watercolor paint. The crayon will show through the paint, so choose paint colors that are different from the crayon color.

15

● WATERCOLOR LEAVES

1. Place a leaf on your paper and hold it down. Paint around the outside edge of the leaf with any color you like.

2. Remove the leaf and let the paint dry. Paint the inside leaf shape with a different color. Let it dry.

3. Draw the leaf's veins with a felt-tip pen.

MORE IDEAS!

● MAKE A FUN PLACEMAT

If you use a large piece of paper your leaf painting, you can make placemat by covering it with cle contact paper.

● **THIS IS A RUBBING** of the leaf used on page 14.

● **A PRETTY CARD** for a special person can be made from this leaf print.

● **CHOOSE SEVERAL LEAVES** and overlap them, using a different colored crayon for each.

● **BOOKMARKS** are fun to try, too!

Just Picture It!

YOUR PICTURES WILL LOOK BETTER when they're in a picture frame made with things you've gathered from the great outdoors. Paint an old frame your favorite color and decorate it with shells, rocks, moss, nuts or seeds.

● **THIS IS** a great way to use your shell collection.

SUPPLIES

picture frame

tempera or
acrylic paint

white glue or
tacky glue

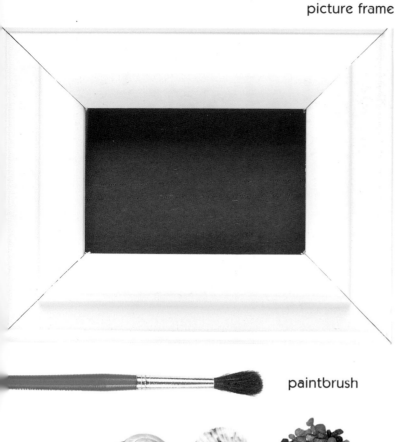

paintbrush

natural
materials

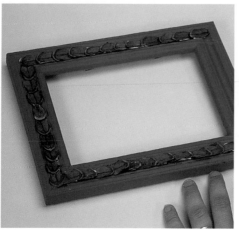

If you want your frame to be a different color, paint it.

2. Put glue on the frame and add your natural materials, such as these pinecone pieces.

3. We added moss and sun-flower seeds. See what you can find to put on your frame!

Nature Tiles

THESE TILES ARE EASY TO MAKE with air-dry clay and pebbles, shells, seeds and fresh leaves and flowers. Make a name plaque to hang in your locker or on your bedroom door.

● HOLIDAYS AND BIRTHDAYS are perfect times to give these tiles as gifts.

KIDS! Try this!

Use cookie cutters to make tiles in different shapes and sizes.

SUPPLIES

air-dry clay

fresh leaves,
flowers, shells,
pebbles

paper or
cardboard

You also need:

- drinking straw
- cookie cutter

paintbrush

rolling pin or glass
with straight sides

decoupage
medium

tip

White glue mixed
with a little water can be
used in place of decoupage
medium.

dull knife

. Use a glass with smooth
straight sides or a rolling pin
flatten your clay on a piece of
cardboard or paper. The clay
should be about ¼" (6.4mm) thick.

2. Cut the clay in the shape you
want by pressing it with a
drinking glass or cookie cutter. For a
square or rectangle, slice it with a
dull knife.

3. Decorate your tile with your
natural objects. Leaves and
flowers can be fresh because they
will be sealed by the decoupage
medium or glue.

21

4. Gently press the objects into the clay with your finger.

5. If you want to hang up your tile, poke a hole in the top with a straw.

6. Paint the front of the tile with decoupage medium or white glue mixed with a little water. Leave it flat until it's dry, about 24 hours.

MORE IDEAS!

• **YOUR TILE CAN BE LONG AND SKINNY.** This shape works well if you want to spell your name in rocks or shells.

● **THE BEAUTY OF FALL** can last all year long when you paint your leaf tiles. Decoupage medium helps to keep the leaf colors bright.

● **ADD A HOLE** to hang your tile. This tile has the initials PH on it. Make one with your own initials.

● **CHOOSE BRIGHT LEAVES** and rocks of different shapes for a pretty mix of colors and textures.

23

Twiggy Creations

TWIGS CAN BE USED TO MAKE so many different projects. Make a fish skeleton plaque or a pencil holder decorated with beads, shells or small rocks. Then think of other twig creations you can make!

● **YOUR FISH CAN BE** long and skinny or short and fat. Try changing the size or length of your twigs.

DON'T FORGET...

Never tear branches and twigs off of living trees. Always use twigs and sticks you find on the ground.

SUPPLIES

paintbrush

white glue
or tacky glue

cardboard

fresh or
pressed leaves

scissors

pebbles, shells, or
other decorations

sticks

1. The fish's body is a long stick. Break some sticks into small [pie]ces and glue them to the long [stick] with the shorter ones on the [end.] Use plenty of glue. Use a thick [stick] for the tail.

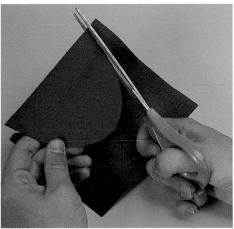

2. Cut a half circle of cardboard for the head.

3. Glue layers of fresh leaves to the cardboard.

25

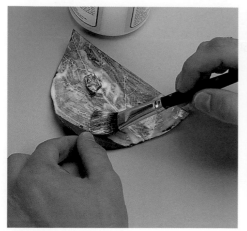

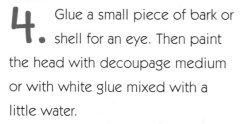

4. Glue a small piece of bark or shell for an eye. Then paint the head with decoupage medium or with white glue mixed with a little water.

5. After the glue is dry, glue the head onto the fish skeleton.

6. You may need to prop a twig behind the head to keep it in place until it's dry. When all the glue is dry, hang your fish skeleton on a wall!

MORE IDEAS!

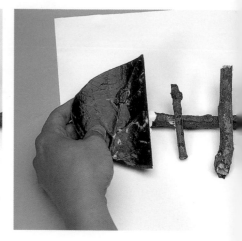

● START WITH A FEW TWIG and add wire, seed beads and a fe rocks to make ornaments. Add a l of string to hang your ornament from a rearview mirror in a car o on a tree.

● **NATURAL ORNAMENTS** are not only beautiful, they are recyclable, too. Just throw them in a leaf pile when you're finished with them.

● **THIS PENCIL HOLDER** was made by gluing sticks to an empty toilet tissue tube. Raffia, a clay bead and a feather make it special. See page 42 to learn how to make clay beads.

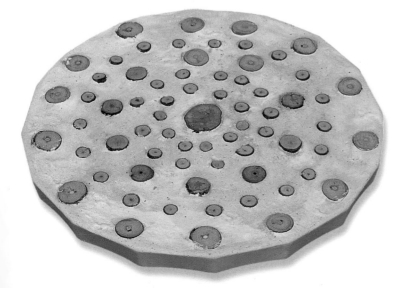

● **TRIVETS ARE HANDY** for holding hot pots and dishes. This one was made by pouring plaster into a plastic deli container, then pressing the round twig pieces into it. An adult must saw the pieces for you.

27

Blooming Cornhusks

YEARS AGO, LITTLE GIRLS MADE cornhusk dolls. And no wonder—crafting with cornhusks is fun! These flowers can be made in a rainbow of colors and they'll never wilt.

• **THESE BRIGHT PETALS** got their color from powdered drink mix! Stir a packet of drink mix into a cup of hot water. Soak your corn husks until they are bright then let them dry.

DRYING CORNHUSKS

Dried cornhusks for tamales are sold at grocery stores. You can make your own by shucking the green husk from an ear of corn and letting it dry in the sun for five to seven days until it turns light yellow.

SUPPLIES

paintbrush

straight stick or pencil

cup of water

watercolors

cornhusks

white glue

raffia or string

scissors

1. Soak the cornhusks in a cup of water for about 30 minutes to ~~soft~~en them.

2. Paint the husks with watercolors and let them dry.

3. Cut the cornhusks into rectangles and stack them in groups of three or four.

4. Fold all the rectangles together like a fan.

5. Tie a piece of raffia or string around the middle and knot it.

6. Open the folds on each en to make the petals.

Make **a whole bouquet** of cornhusk flowers. They will **last forever** and never need wat

7. Fold the cornhusk in half and tie it with a long piece of raffia or string to finish the flower.

8. Use raffia to tie the flower onto a pencil or stick to form a stem.

9. Paint cornhusk strips green and wrap them around the stick or pencil. Glue the ends wit white glue.

• **CORNHUSK FLOWERS** were tied to a long piece of raffia to make this necklace or headband.

A BEAUTIFUL ANGEL can be made from a ~~wo~~oden clothespin and cornhusk pieces for clothing. ~~Th~~e angel's hair is a piece of wool dyed with tea. ~~Th~~e angel was painted with watercolors.

• **WEAVE STRIPS OF CORNHUSKS** and glue the woven squares to a piece of burlap to make these natural looking placemats. Make a matching coaster and add a sticker to both.

Wild Impressions

Take this nature sack to bag your "treasures" as you hik through the forest or stroll on the beach. Anything that can be coated with paint can be used for printing: flower ferns, shells, feathers, leaves, an even rocks.

tip

Never take anything from nature that is an animal's home. Also remember to only take what you think you will use and return all leftover natural materials back to nature.

SUPPLIES

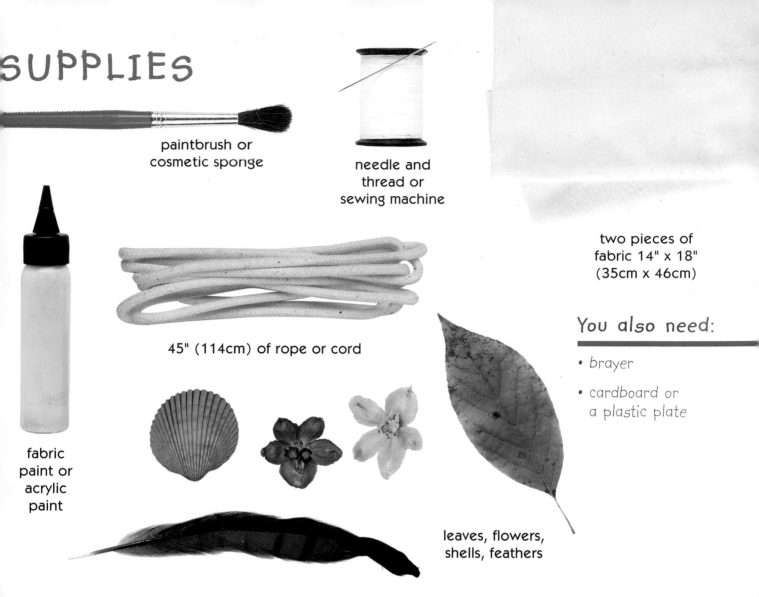

paintbrush or cosmetic sponge

needle and thread or sewing machine

45" (114cm) of rope or cord

fabric paint or acrylic paint

leaves, flowers, shells, feathers

two pieces of fabric 14" x 18" (35cm x 46cm)

You also need:

- brayer
- cardboard or a plastic plate

Squirt fabric or acrylic paint on a piece of cardboard or a plastic plate.

2. Use a paintbrush or cosmetic sponge to put the paint on the item you want to print. The sponge makes prints with more details; the paintbrush makes bolder-looking prints.

3. Lay the item paint side down on the fabric. Put a piece of paper on top of it and rub it with your hands or roll it with a brayer. Try to keep the item from moving when you do this.

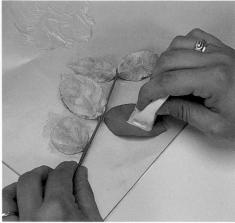

4. Carefully remove the item. You can put more paint on it and print it again or choose something else.

5. Choose a new color and put the paint on another item. Keep printing on both pieces of fabric until you are happy with the way it looks.

6. Let the paint dry for at least an hour. Put your pieces of fabric on top of each other, with painted sides touching. Sew three sides together ½" (1.27cm) from the edge. You can use a sewing machine or a needle and thread.

Take this sack with you when you go for a walk to carry home your treasures

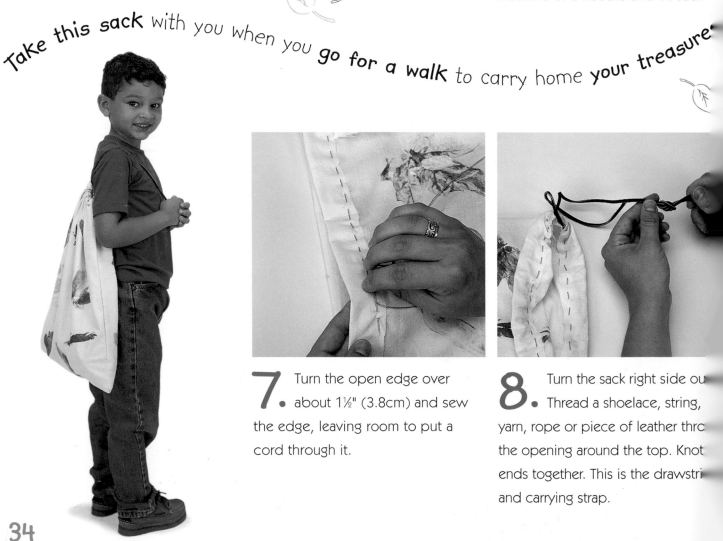

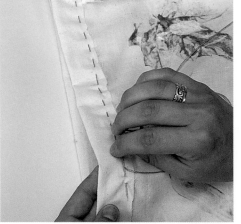

7. Turn the open edge over about 1½" (3.8cm) and sew the edge, leaving room to put a cord through it.

8. Turn the sack right side out. Thread a shoelace, string, yarn, rope or piece of leather through the opening around the top. Knot ends together. This is the drawstring and carrying strap.

34

MORE IDEAS!

• **MAKING A PILLOW** is even easier than making a sack. Sew all the way around the edges, leaving an opening in one side. Turn the pillow right side out and stuff it. Then sew up the hole.

• **FOR A PAPERWEIGHT** or garden decoration you can print ferns, flowers or leaves on rocks.

• **AT YOUR NEXT CAMP-OUT** you can decorate your pillowcase using leaves you find in the woods.

Nature Bangles

Here's a great party activity! You can make attractive bracelets with plastic tubing filled with beads, colored sand, tiny shells or birdseed. The tubing is sold in the plumbing section of hardware stores or in the aquarium section of pet stores.

● **A MATCHING NECKLACE** to go with these bracelets can be made with a longer piece of tubing.

SUPPLIES

- small seeds, beads or shells
- spoon

clear plastic tubing ⅜" and ¼"(10mm and 6.4mm) inner diameter

scissors

sand

cup

liquid food coloring

1. Mix the sand and food coloring in separate cups or pour into plastic bags and shake. Mix several colors if you like.

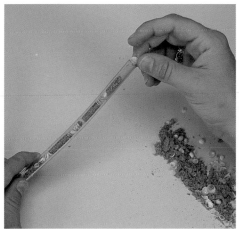

2. Use scissors to cut a piece of the ⅜" (10mm) tubing to fit your wrist. Hold your thumb over the bottom end of the tube. Pour the sand into the other end. Add shells, beads, pebbles or other small things.

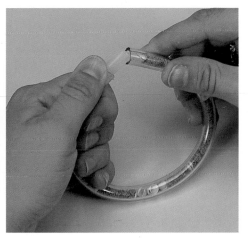

3. Cut a short piece of the ¼" (6.4mm) tubing with scissors. Put this piece inside the two ends of the larger tubing to finish the bracelet.

Keepsake Pillow

Have you ever come home from a trip to the beach with postcards, photos and seashells? Or maybe you have mementos from summer camp when you caught a fish, made new friends and hiked up a mountain. This pillow is made from souvenir you've collected.

SUPPLIES

paintbrush

embroidery floss
or thin yarn and
needle

needle and
thread

fabric
paint or
acrylic
paint

fabric and piece
of clear vinyl

scissors

hole punch

stuffing

KIDS! Try this!

HERE ARE FUN THINGS you
can put in your keepsake pillow:

- camp or vacation photos
- shells or feathers
- a postcard or drawing

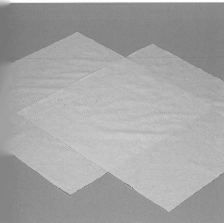

Cut two pieces of fabric the
● size you want for your pillow.
s one is 14" (35cm) square.

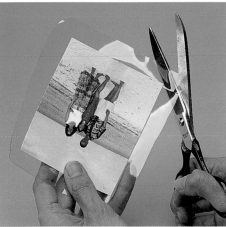

2. Choose a favorite photo for
your pillow. Cut a piece of
vinyl about 2" (5cm) larger than your
photo. Vinyl can be bought by the
yard at a fabric store.

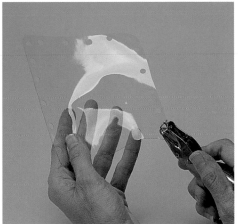

3. Punch holes around three
edges of the vinyl. Place the
holes about 1" (2.5cm) apart and ½"
away from the edge.

39

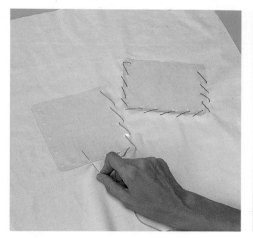

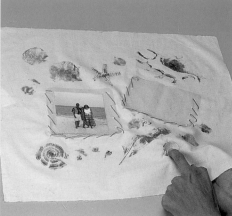

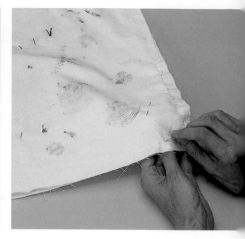

4. Use embroidery floss or thin yarn to sew the vinyl pockets to the fabric. Poke your needle through the holes in the vinyl.

5. Use different colors of fabric or acrylic paint to print your souvenirs onto both sides of the pillow. (*See pages 32-34 for directions.*) Let the paint dry.

6. Put the printed sides of the fabric squares together and sew three of the edges with a sewing machine or with a needle and thread.

Get creative!! Keepsake pillows make **great gifts** *for your* **friends and family!!**

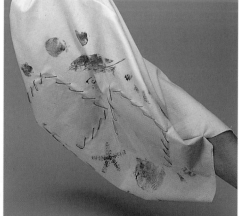

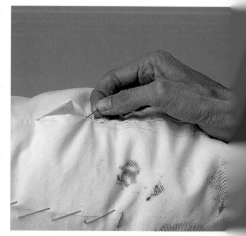

7. Sew in from the ends of the fourth side, leaving a 4" (10cm) opening for the stuffing.

8. Turn the pillow right side out and carefully stuff it with pillow stuffing.

9. Sew the opening closed. P photos or seashells into the vinyl pockets.

● **SUMMER CAMP** is a great place to make a keepsake pillow. You can really put paint on a fish and print it. Your camp friends can autograph your pillow or you can ask them to dip their fingers, hands or feet in paint and make prints on the fabric.

● **THE APPLE PRINT** near the center of this pillow is made with a real cut apple. You can print with vegetables, too!

41

Shells You Wear

WITH THESE CLAY BEADS, you can make necklaces, keychains and bracelets. Try using different size shells or painting the beads after they are baked for a brighter look.

● OVEN-BAKE CLAY in tan or white is sold at craft stores.

SUPPLIES

seashells

cord, elastic,
or leather

wooden skewers

oven-bake clay

HAVE AN
ADULT HELP YOU!

The clay in this project needs
to be baked in a conventional or
toaster oven. Ask an adult to
bake the clay for you and
follow the directions on
the package.

polymer clay

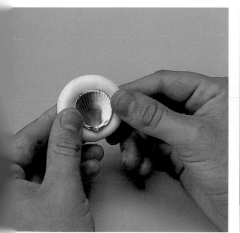

Knead the polymer clay until
it's soft and roll it into a ball.
h a shell into the clay to make a
d for your beads.

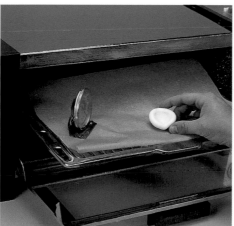

2. Ask an adult to bake the clay
following the directions on
the package. Make more than one
mold if you want to create beads of
different sizes.

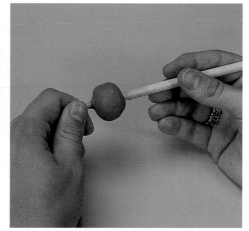

3. After the polymer clay mold
cools roll a ball of oven-bake
clay and put a skewer through it.
Make sure the ball is big enough to
fill the shell mold.

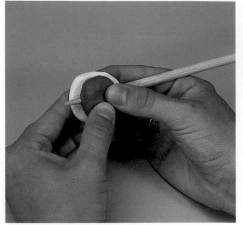
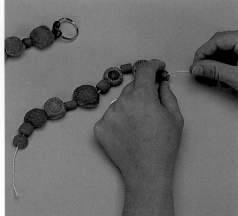

4. With the clay still on the skewer, push it into the shell mold. Remove the bead and slide it off the skewer. Make more beads and let them dry overnight. Ask an adult to bake them in an oven.

5. String the beads on elastic or leather for a bracelet. Use a longer piece of cord or leather to make a matching necklace.

6. To make a keychain, use a slipknot to tie a piece of leather around a metal key ring. Ad four or five beads and tie a knot to hold the beads in place.

Have some fun! Clay bead creations make **great projects** for a rainy day!

● **MANY TYPES** of small shells will make good molds for making beads.

THIS HANDY KEYCHAIN would make a thoughtful gift for teacher or parent.

● **CHANGE THE LOOK** of your necklace by using just a few beads or many.

Plant Pounding

YOU'LL HAVE DOUBLE THE FUN with this project collecting pretty flowers and leaves then pounding the color out of them. Look for bright and colorful flowers such as daisies, zinnias or pansies.

DON'T WASH ME...

Most flower colors fade or disappear in the wash, so you'll want to make projects that won't need washing such as this wall hanging.

SUPPLIES

raffia or yarn

fresh flowers,
ferns and leaves

fabric

dull knife

scissors

stick

masking tape

needle and thread
or thin yarn

hammer

FLOWER BANNER

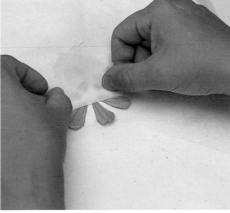

1. Cut your fabric to the size you want for your banner. Lay a ~~flo~~wer or leaf on the fabric.

2. Put masking tape over the entire plant.

3. Flip the fabric over onto a hard surface such as a board. A concrete floor in a basement or garage is also a good place to pound plants.

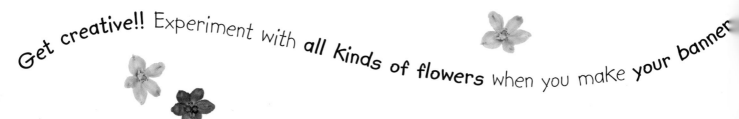

4. Pound the fabric with a hammer until all of the plant's colors come through the fabric. Be careful not to pound too hard or you will rip the fabric.

5. Peel off the masking tape with the plant. Set the fabric aside to dry.

6. Use a dull knife to scrape th fabric clean of all loose plan material.

Get creative!! Experiment with all kinds of flowers when you make your banner

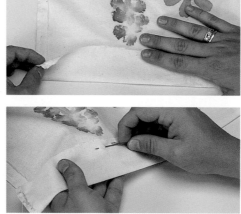

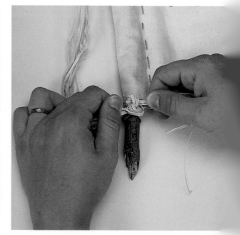

7. Keep pounding flowers, leaves and stems until your fabric is covered.

8. To turn your picture into a banner, fold over the top of the fabric. Sew the edge with thread or thin yarn leaving a space for a stick to slide through.

9. Slide a stick through the top and tie raffia or yarn the ends for hanging.

● **THIS BANNER LOOKS GREAT** hanging in your room. Or make a pretty pillow by pounding flowers, leaves and ferns on two squares of fabric. Then follow the sewing directions on page 40.

● **THE BEST PLANT** to use for t-shirts is a fern because the color may darken but won't wash out the way most flower colors do. After you tape the fern to the front of the shirt, turn it inside out over a board so the color won't come through to the back of the shirt when you pound it.

WASH THIS...

Fern poundings don't wash out, so they are great to use on t-shirts. Try also using ferns to decorate cloth placemats, napkins, or a tablecloth for a great gift!

50

Pound flowers, leaves and stems into a piece of fabric. Cut around the print with scissors.

2. Cut a piece of contact paper slightly larger than your print. Remove the backing and place the contact paper over the flower. Cut around the edges and stick your decal on a window.

• DECALS LOOK BEAUTIFUL in a window because the sun shines through them and lights up the colors. You can also use these flowers and leaves as decorations for greeting cards or wrapped gifts.

51

Balancing Act

A MOBILE IS AN UNUSUAL WAY TO DISPLAY all the nature treasure you've collected. Make your mobile with your own collection of sticks, shells, rocks, pinecones, seed pods and even photographs! Fishing swivels give the mobile more movement, but you can make your mobile without them.

tip

Look for rocks or shells that have natural holes in them. They will be easier to tie to your mobile.

SUPPLIES

natural materials

scissors

white glue or tacky glue

yarn or string

sticks

You also need

• craft wire

KIDS! **Try this!**

FISHING SWIVELS will make your mobile turn with just the slightest breeze. They can be found in stores that carry fishing tackle. **FUN!**

1. Find a place to hang your mobile while you are working it. Use the back of a chair, a kitchen counter or stack up two stacks of books and put a stick between them.

2. Start tying objects together. This shell has a natural hole just right for string to fit through.

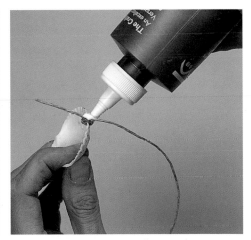

3. Put a dot of white glue or tacky glue on your knots before cutting the string.

53

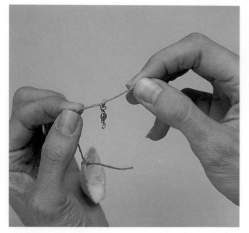

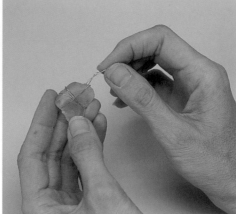

4. If you want your mobile to move more, tie fishing swivels at the top of your mobile strands. Remember, it's not necessary to do this.

5. Wrap solid objects (such as this piece of sea glass) with wire and make a loop for hanging. Other items such as acorns and pinecones can be glued to the end of the yarn or string.

6. When you have made sever[al] strands, start tying them ont[o] short sticks.

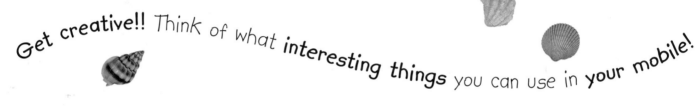

Get creative!! Think of what interesting things you can use in **your mobile!**

7. After you've tied two or more strands to a short stick, tie a piece of string in the center. Move the center string from side to side until the stick hangs straight. This stick is not yet straight.

8. When the stick hangs straight, like this one, it is balanced. Choose a long stick for the top of your mobile and hang two or more of these short balanced sticks from it.

9. Every time you add something to the mobile, the strings need to be adjusted so all the sticks balance. Your mobile c[an] be as large or small as you like.

- **A NATURE HIKE** in the woods offers plenty of material for a mobile. Try hanging your mobile outside or near a window where the breeze will make it move.

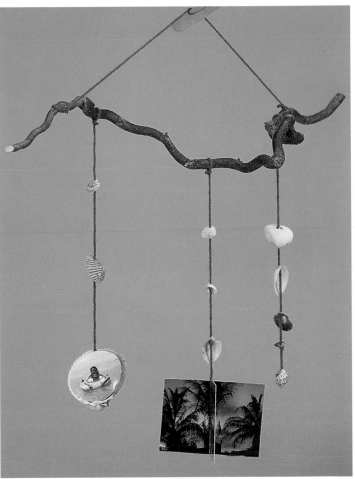

- **VACATION MEMORIES** can be added to any mobile. This mobile has two post-cards. One postcard was cut from the bottom up the center halfway. The other was cut from the top down the center halfway. The cards were fitted together and a piece of yarn was glued where they both cross.

Pebble Mosaics

Mosaics are pictures made from bits of broken materials. This project is much easier to do because you use pebbles to make the design. These rocks make great doorstops or paperweights. You can also use pebbles to decorate candle holders, picture frames, ceramic tiles, even small cardboard boxes.

DARK PEBBLES used as a background make the light pebbles in each picture show up best.

SUPPLIES

large rock

pebbles or
small shells

pencil

white glue or
tacky glue

KIDS! Try this!

Make a **MINI MOSAIC VALENTINE** with a small heart-shaped rock.

tip

Try tacky Glue! It is easier to use for gluing bumpy things because it is thicker than white glue.

1. Draw a picture or write your name on the rock with a pencil or felt-tip pen.

2. Squeeze a line of glue on part of the picture. Put a line of pebbles into the glue so that they touch each other. Use a little glue at a time so it doesn't dry before you place all the pebbles.

3. Fill in the inside shape and then do the background with a different kind of pebble. The light pebbles show up well against the dark background.

57

Glowing Flowers

project 15

WHEN YOU PRESS FLOWERS AND LEAVES, they become thinner and light can shine through them. In this project, you simply glue paper and pressed flowers and leaves to a glass candle holder. When the candle is lit, the flowers will glow!

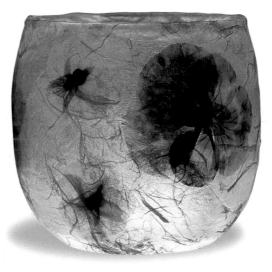

● THESE COLORFUL CANDLE HOLDERS were made with thin handmade paper from a craft store.

CHECK THIS OUT...

Page 11 has directions for pressing your own flowers.

SUPPLIES

pressed
flowers
and leaves

thin paper

glass votive

decoupage medium

paintbrush

tip

White glue mixed with a
little water can be used in
place of decoupage medium.

1. Tear off all the straight edges
from a sheet of tissue paper,
then tear the paper into small pieces.
You can use any kind of paper that is
thin enough to let light shine through.

2. Brush the glass candle holder
with decoupage medium or
white glue mixed with water. Arrange
the pressed flowers and leaves all
around the glass.

3. Brush on more glue and lay
the pieces of paper on the
glass, overlapping the edges. Keep
adding paper and glue until the
glass is covered.

Treasure Dish

WHERE DO YOU PUT ALL THE SMALL THINGS that you collect in your pockets? This treasure dish will hold your lucky stone, special shell and other small stuff. A big shell or leaf makes the best dish.

SUPPLIES

rolling pin or
straight-sided
drinking glass

paper

oven-bake
clay

shell, rock or
large leaf

baking sheet

dull knife

SHELL DISH

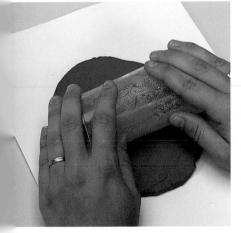

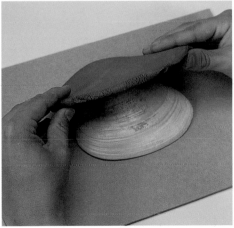

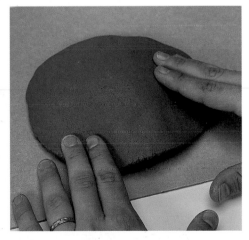

Use a smooth drinking glass with straight sides or a rolling to roll out a slab of clay on a ce of paper. It should be about (3mm) thick and larger than the m you're using as a mold.

2. Place your slab of clay over the shell or rock.

3. Press the clay against the shell with your fingers until the clay touches all of the shell.

4. Use a dull knife to trim off the extra clay around the top edge of the shell. If you're using a rock, cut the clay evenly around the rock to make the top edge of your dish.

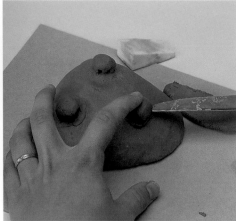

5. Roll little clay balls for feet. Put the balls in place and use a dull knife, popsicle stick or your finger to smooth away the seam line. This will keep the feet from falling off later.

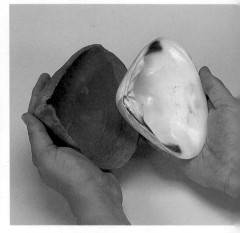

6. Let the clay dry for about an hour until it becomes stiff. Carefully take out the shell or rock and let the clay dry overnight. Have an adult bake the clay in an oven once the clay is completely dry. Follow the package directions.

LEAF DISH

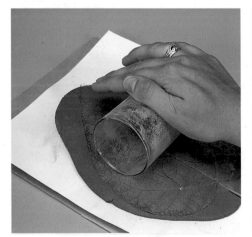

1. Roll out a clay slab, place a leaf on the clay and gently press it into the clay with a rolling pin or glass.

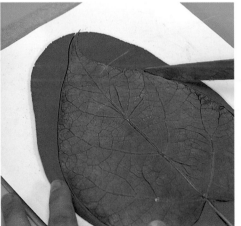

2. Use a dull knife to cut around the leaf. Make clay balls for the feet.

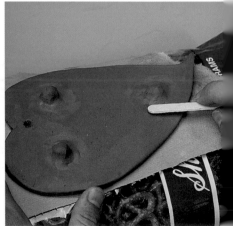

3. Put your leaf face down on something curved, such as rolled up towel or even a bag of pretzels. Add the clay feet as shown above in step 5. Let the clay dry overnight and ask an adult to bake the leaf following the directions on the package of clay.

- **THIS DISH WAS MADE** by pressing the clay around a large rock. Be sure to remove the rock as soon as the clay is stiff but not yet dry or the rock may not come out!

- **A PRETTY, CURVY SHELL** was used to make this dish.

- **DECORATE YOUR LEAF** dish with a small branch attached with a ball of clay.

63

More fun books for CREATIVE KIDS!

Try these fun, no-mess projects inspired by your favorite stories, including *How Many Bugs in a Box, I Wish I Were a Butterfly, Gingerbread Baby* and more. You'll learn how to make soft felt boxes, lace-wing butterfly barrettes, a milk carton gingerbread house and other exciting creations. There are 26 projects in each volume!

Volume 1: ISBN 1-58180-059-2, paperback, 128 pages, #31622-K

Volume 2: ISBN 1-58180-088-6, paperback, 128 pages, #31688-K

Oh, the things you can create with paper! Learn how to make paper stars, party streamers, lanterns, hanging baskets, paper beads, hand-made books, decoupage and more. These crafts are perfect for parties, rainy days and gift giving, plus they're easy to do and fun to make.

ISBN 1-58180-290-0, paperback, 64 pages, #32167-K

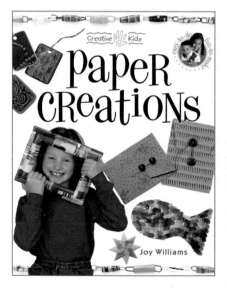

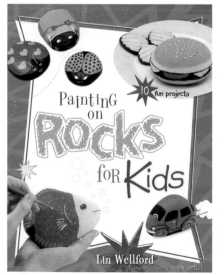

Create amazing creatures, incredible toys and wild gifts for your friends and family. All it takes is some paint, a few rocks and your imagination! Easy-to-follow pictures and instructions show you how to turn simple stones into something cool—racecars, bugs, lizards, teddy bears and more.

ISBN 1-58180-255-2, paperback, 64 pages, #32085-K

These and other great North Light books are available at your favorite arts & crafts store, bookstore or library. You or your parents can call 1-800-289-0963 for more information!